steam it!

steam it!

for meals that taste the way nature intended

MARKS & SPENCER

Marks and Spencer p.l.c.
PO Box 3339
Chester CH99 9QS

shop online
www.marksandspencer.com

ISBN: 978-1-84805-402-8

Printed in China

Recipes and introduction written by Linda Doeser
Designed by Andrew Easton at Ummagumma
Photography by Charlie Richards
Food styling by Lucy Jessop

Notes for the Reader

This book uses both metric and imperial measurements. Follow the same units of measurement throughout; do not mix metric and imperial. All spoon measurements are level: teaspoons are assumed to be 5 ml, and tablespoons are assumed to be 15 ml. Unless otherwise stated, milk is assumed to be full fat, eggs and individual vegetables are medium, and pepper is freshly ground black pepper.

The times given are an approximate guide only. Preparation times differ according to the techniques used by different people and the cooking times may also vary from those given. Optional ingredients, variations or serving suggestions have not been included in the calculations.

Recipes using raw or very lightly cooked eggs should be avoided by infants, the elderly, pregnant women, convalescents and anyone suffering from an illness. Pregnant and breastfeeding women are advised to avoid eating peanuts and peanut products. Sufferers from nut allergies should be aware that some of the ready-made ingredients used in the recipes in this book may contain nuts. Always check the packaging before use.

contents

introduction

Far more kinds of foods can be cooked by the gentle method of steaming than most people realize – from vegetable medleys to layered terrines, from whole fish to hearty hotpots and from fluffy grains to creamy desserts. Forget any preconceptions about stodgy suet puddings and discover that winter warmers, whether sweet or savoury, can be light and airy as well as full of flavour.

Steaming is the perfect technique for today's health-conscious and busy cooks. It retains far more nutrients than other methods of cooking and does not require added fat or oil. The colour and texture of ingredients are retained and it is an ideal way of cooking delicate foods, such as fish. Although not invariably the case, many types of food, such as fresh

vegetables, seafood and thin cuts of meat, are cooked extremely quickly and, as you can stack steamers over each other, it can also be very economical with fuel.

Steaming methods

A traditional method of steaming is to put the ingredients directly into a steamer – a perforated metal container – cover with a tight-fitting lid and set it over a saucepan of boiling water. This simple technique is still a useful one for lots of foods. However, for extra flavour, other liquids, such as stock or reserved marinade, may be substituted for water and these can then sometimes be used as the basis for a sauce to serve with the dish. Adding aromatic herbs, spices or citrus rind to plain water also enhances the flavour of the food.

A second classic method of steaming is to put the food in a container, such as a pudding basin, heatproof dish or ramekin, cover it with greaseproof paper and/or foil and put this in the steamer. Traditional sweet and savoury suet crust pies and sponge desserts are cooked this way and it also works well for stews, mixed vegetable dishes, fruit and egg custards.

A variation of this method is to stand the covered basin on an upturned plate or a trivet inside a large saucepan of boiling water. This prevents it from being in direct contact with the heat source. Make sure that the water comes no more than halfway up the side of the container and that there is plenty of room for the steam to circulate. Remember to cover the pan.

Ingredients that require a longer cooking time, such as thick cuts of meat and whole fish, need extra protection as otherwise they may dry out in spite of the moist atmosphere in the steamer. Wrapping the food in a greaseproof paper or foil parcel keeps it moist and seals in the nutrients and flavour. You can also use a variety of leaves for wrapping, such as chard, lettuce, banana or corn husks, some of which are edible and all of which look appealing.

Rice and other grains are usually steamed in a slightly different way. The rice and a measured

quantity of cold water are put into a saucepan so that the rice is covered by about 2.5 cm/1 inch. When the water comes to the boil, the heat is reduced to a simmer, the pan is covered with a tight-fitting lid and the rice is left to steam for 15–20 minutes, until all the liquid has been absorbed. The pan is then removed from the heat and allowed to stand for a few minutes, still covered, to finish steaming. Live shellfish, such as mussels and clams, are steamed in a similar way, although with less liquid and for a shorter time.

Types of steamer

Almost all steamers require three components: a container for the boiling liquid, usually a saucepan or wok, a steaming compartment and a tight-fitting lid.

• Tiered steamers are usually made of aluminium, have a perforated base and are designed with a series of graduated ridges on the base to fit a wide variety of saucepan sizes. They may be stacked so that different ingredients can be steamed simultaneously. They are often supplied with a domed lid. Electrical models are also available with a thermostatically controlled heating element under the bottom container for the liquid.

• Flexible steamers are usually made of steel with adjustable folding sides and short legs that stand on the base of a saucepan. They come in a range of sizes to fit most saucepans and are very adaptable. Make sure that the saucepan has a tight-fitting lid.

• Bamboo steamers are designed to rest against the side of a wok about 5 cm/2 inches above the water level. These attractive Chinese baskets can be stacked in a tower and are supplied with a tight-fitting bamboo lid. They are available from Asian supermarkets and stores.

Dos and don'ts

- Do not let the boiling liquid touch the steaming compartment.
- Do not let the liquid boil dry. Check the level every 15–20 minutes and top up with boiling water or stock, as required.
- Do ensure you always cover the steamer with a tight-fitting lid.
- Do keep an eye on the cooking time, as the heat during steaming is intense and it is easy to overcook. Become familiar with your own steamer: timings given in the recipes are guidelines only.
- Do not leave food in the steamer after cooking, even with the heat turned off, as it will continue to cook and, possibly, spoil.

fish & shellfish

rolled fillets of sole

SERVES 4

4 sole, filleted and skinned
2 tbsp olive oil
1 tbsp white wine vinegar
2 tbsp finely chopped fresh parsley
1 courgette, grated
1 carrot, grated
1 onion, very finely chopped
4 tbsp fresh white breadcrumbs
1 tbsp lemon juice
425 ml/15 fl oz fish stock
150 ml/5 fl oz white wine
salt and pepper
fresh parsley sprigs, to garnish

Put the sole fillets into a shallow, non-metallic dish. Mix together the oil, vinegar and parsley and pour the mixture over the fish. Cover with clingfilm and leave to marinate for 30 minutes.

Mix together the courgette, carrot, onion, breadcrumbs and lemon juice in a bowl and season to taste with salt and pepper.

Pour the fish stock and white wine into a saucepan and bring to the boil. Meanwhile, drain the fish, pat dry with kitchen paper and season with salt and pepper. Divide the vegetable stuffing evenly between the fish fillets and roll up. Place the fish rolls in a single layer in a heatproof dish that will fit inside the steamer.

Place the steamer over the pan of boiling stock and cover with a tight-fitting lid. Steam for about 8 minutes, until the flesh flakes easily. Remove from the steamer and serve immediately, garnished with parsley sprigs.

chinese steamed sea bream

SERVES 4

1 sea bream, about 1 kg/2 lb 4 oz, scaled and cleaned
1 tsp salt
2 garlic cloves, finely chopped
1 bunch of spring onions, shredded
2 tbsp grated fresh ginger
pinch of caster sugar
$1\frac{1}{2}$ tbsp sesame oil
$1\frac{1}{2}$ tbsp groundnut oil
chopped spring onion and lemon slices, to garnish
light soy sauce, to serve

Bring a saucepan of water to the boil. Meanwhile, rinse the fish well under cold running water and pat dry with kitchen paper. Slash the flesh diagonally several times on both sides and rub in the salt. Put the fish in a heatproof dish or on a deep plate that will fit inside the steamer.

Tuck the garlic, one third of the spring onions and half the ginger inside the cavity of the fish. Place the dish in the steamer and cover with a tight-fitting lid.

Set the steamer over the pan of boiling water and steam for about 20 minutes, until the flesh flakes easily.

Remove the dish from the steamer and sprinkle the fish with the sugar, remaining spring onions and remaining ginger.

Heat the sesame oil and groundnut oil in a small saucepan and, when hot, gently pour the mixture over the fish. Serve immediately, garnished with chopped spring onion and lemon slices and accompanied by a small dish of light soy sauce.

monkfish in swiss chard parcels

SERVES 4

500 g/1 lb 2 oz Swiss chard, trimmed
550 g/1 lb 4 oz monkfish fillet, cut into bite-sized pieces
1½ tbsp lime juice
150 ml/5 fl oz crème fraîche
2 egg yolks, lightly beaten
pinch of paprika
40 g/1½ oz butter
125 ml/4 fl oz white wine
salt and pepper

Cut the stems from the chard leaves and reserve. Steam 8 leaves for 15 seconds, then remove and spread out on a work surface. Shred any remaining leaves.

Mix together the pieces of fish, lime juice and 5 tablespoons of the crème fraîche in a bowl. Stir in the egg yolks, add the paprika and season to taste.

Divide the fish mixture equally between the steamed leaves, then roll up, tucking in the sides. Secure with cocktail sticks or tie with kitchen string.

Bring a saucepan of water to the boil and line a steamer with greaseproof paper. Put the rolls in the steamer in a single layer, cover with a tight-fitting lid and steam for 15–20 minutes, until tender.

Meanwhile, finely chop the reserved chard stalks. Melt the butter in frying pan, add the stalks and cook over a low heat, stirring occasionally, for 10 minutes, until tender. Stir in the white wine and bring to the boil.

Transfer the chard stem mixture to a blender or food processor, add the remaining crème fraîche and process until smooth. Scrape the mixture into a saucepan, add the shredded chard leaves and cook over a low heat, stirring constantly, until thickened. Season to taste.

Remove the fish parcels from the steamer. Remove and discard the cocktail sticks or kitchen string and transfer to a serving dish. Spoon the sauce into the dish and serve immediately.

marinated salmon with chilli sauce

SERVES 4

4 salmon fillets, about
175 g/6 oz each
4 spring onions, chopped
1 lemon grass stalk, chopped
1 tbsp finely chopped fresh ginger
2 fresh red chillies, deseeded and finely chopped
2 tbsp Thai fish sauce
fresh coriander sprigs, to garnish

marinade
juice of 1 lime
2 tbsp Chinese rice wine or dry sherry
3 tbsp chopped fresh coriander
2 garlic cloves, finely chopped

chilli sauce
12 fresh red chillies, deseeded and coarsely chopped
3 garlic cloves, finely chopped
1 tbsp soft brown sugar
juice of 1 lime
4 tbsp Thai fish sauce

Put the salmon fillets in a shallow dish. Mix together all the marinade ingredients and pour over the fish. Turn to coat, cover with clingfilm and leave to marinate for 30 minutes.

Meanwhile, make the chilli sauce. Put all the ingredients into a food processor or blender and process until thoroughly blended. Scrape the sauce into a small serving bowl and set aside until required.

Bring a saucepan of water to the boil. Meanwhile, line a steamer with greaseproof paper. Drain the salmon fillets, reserving the marinade, and put them in the steamer in a single layer. Add the spring onions, lemon grass, ginger, chillies and Thai fish sauce to the reserved marinade and mix well. Spoon the mixture evenly over the fish.

Cover the steamer with a tight-fitting lid and set it over the pan of boiling water. Steam for 10 minutes, until the fish flakes easily.

Lift out the fish fillets from the steamer and put them onto warmed serving plates. Garnish with coriander sprigs and serve immediately with the chilli sauce.

seafood & lemon grass skewers

SERVES 4

8 lemon grass stalks
1 tbsp groundnut oil
2 tbsp lemon juice
1 tbsp finely chopped fresh mint
1 tsp green peppercorns
24 raw tiger prawns, peeled and deveined
12 large scallops, shucked and halved
300 ml/10 fl oz water
salt and pepper
fresh mint sprigs, to garnish

Remove the outer leaves from the lemon grass stalks. Cut off and finely chop the bulbous base of the stalks and put into a bowl. Reserve the stalks. Add the oil, lemon juice, chopped mint and peppercorns to the bowl, mix well and season with salt and pepper.

Thread the prawns and scallops alternately onto the lemon grass stalks and place in a large, shallow non-metallic dish. Pour the marinade over them and turn to coat. Cover with clingfilm and set aside in a cool place for 30 minutes.

Line a steamer with greaseproof paper. Drain the skewers, reserving the marinade, and put into the steamer. Cover with a tight-fitting lid. Pour the marinade into a saucepan, add the water and bring to the boil. Set the steamer over the pan and steam for 10 minutes, until the seafood is cooked through and tender.

Remove the skewers from the steamer and serve immediately, garnished with mint sprigs.

shellfish medley with radicchio cream

SERVES 4

300 ml/10 fl oz fish stock
450 g/1 lb live mussels
225 g/8 oz live clams
12 raw tiger prawns
115 g/4 oz mangetout
12 baby carrots, trimmed
½ mooli, sliced
8 scallops, shucked and halved
4 tbsp lemon juice
2 tbsp chopped fresh parsley
1 head of radicchio, coarsely chopped
3 tbsp crème fraîche
salt and pepper
fresh parsley sprigs, to garnish

Put the stock into a saucepan and bring to the boil. Scrub the mussels and clams under cold running water and pull off the 'beards' from the mussels. Discard any shellfish with damaged shells or that do not shut when sharply tapped.

Put the prawns into a steamer, cover with a tight-fitting lid and set over the pan of boiling stock. Steam for 5 minutes, then remove from the heat and leave to cool slightly. Peel the prawns and add the shells and heads to the stock. Bring the stock back to the boil, reduce the heat and simmer for 10 minutes. Devein the prawns, then halve and set aside.

Remove the heads and shells from the stock. Put the mangetout, carrots and mooli into the steamer, cover with a tight-fitting lid, set over the pan and steam for 5 minutes.

Add all the shellfish to the steamer and sprinkle with the lemon juice and parsley. Re-cover and steam for a further 5 minutes. Transfer the shellfish medley to a dish and keep warm. Discard any mussels or clams that remain closed.

Add the radicchio to the stock, increase the heat to high and boil rapidly until the liquid has reduced by half. Remove the pan from the heat and leave to cool slightly, then transfer the mixture to a blender or food processor. Add the crème fraîche and process until smooth. Season to taste with salt and pepper.

Pour the sauce into a warmed serving dish. Top with the shellfish medley, garnish with parsley sprigs and serve immediately.

prawn wraps with spicy salsa

SERVES 4–6

450 g/1 lb cooked peeled prawns
4 tbsp lime juice
2 tbsp chopped fresh coriander
1 fresh red chilli, deseeded and finely chopped
150 ml/5 fl oz soured cream
1 bunch of spring onions, finely chopped
4 mixed red and yellow peppers, deseeded and finely chopped
4 courgettes, diced
225 g/8 oz baby sweetcorn, thickly sliced
8–12 flour tortillas
salt and pepper

spicy salsa
2 avocados
4 spring onions, finely chopped
4 fresh red chillies, deseeded and finely chopped
2 tbsp olive oil
4 tbsp lime juice
2 tbsp chopped fresh coriander

Put the prawns into a bowl. Mix together the lime juice, half the coriander and the chilli. Pour the mixture over the prawns, stir gently, cover and leave to marinate for 30 minutes.

Mix the soured cream and spring onions together in a small bowl, cover and set aside.

Bring a saucepan of water to the boil. Put the red and yellow peppers, courgettes and sweetcorn in a steamer, cover with a tight-fitting lid and set over the pan of boiling water. Steam for 5 minutes.

Drain the prawns, add to the vegetables, re-cover the steamer and steam for a further 3–5 minutes.

Meanwhile, heat the tortillas. Stack and warm through in a preheated oven at 190°C/375°F/Gas Mark 5 for 5 minutes or heat individually in a preheated heavy frying pan.

Transfer the prawn and vegetable mixture to a warmed serving dish, season to taste with salt and pepper and keep warm while you make the salsa.

Halve and stone the avocados. Scoop out the flesh, dice finely and put into a bowl. Add the spring onions and chillies. Whisk together the olive oil, lime juice and coriander in a jug and pour the dressing over the avocado mixture. Toss gently to mix, and serve immediately as an accompaniment to the tortillas.

mussels steamed in vermouth

SERVES 4

2 tbsp olive oil
6 large shallots, finely chopped
2 garlic cloves, finely chopped
2 fennel bulbs, finely chopped
2 kg/4 lb 8 oz live mussels
300 ml/10 fl oz dry vermouth, such as Noilly Prat
pepper
French bread, to serve

Heat the oil in a large saucepan. Add the shallots, garlic and fennel, cover and cook over a low heat, stirring occasionally, for 8–10 minutes, until soft.

Meanwhile, scrub the mussels under cold running water and pull off the 'beards.' Discard any with broken or damaged shells and any that do not shut immediately when sharply tapped.

Pour the vermouth into the pan and season with pepper. Bring to the boil, add the mussels, cover and cook over a medium-high heat, gently shaking the pan occasionally, for about 5 minutes, until the mussels have opened. Discard any that remain closed.

Divide the contents of the pan between individual soup bowls and serve immediately with French bread.

meat &
poultry

meatballs with tomato & thyme sauce

SERVES 4

1 tbsp olive oil
½ red onion, finely chopped
2 garlic cloves, finely chopped
450 g/1 lb lean steak mince
25 g/1 oz fresh white breadcrumbs
1 egg, lightly beaten
cornflour, for dusting
salt and pepper
freshly cooked spaghetti, to serve (optional)

tomato sauce
400 g/14 oz canned chopped tomatoes
150 ml/5 fl oz beef stock
2 tsp chopped fresh thyme
1 garlic clove, finely chopped
pinch of sugar
salt and pepper

Heat the oil in a frying pan. Add the onion and garlic and cook over a low heat, stirring occasionally, for 5 minutes, until soft. Remove the pan from the heat and transfer the onion and garlic to a bowl.

Add the minced steak, breadcrumbs and egg, season with salt and pepper and mix well until thoroughly combined. Dust your hands with cornflour and shape the mixture into 4-cm/1½-inch balls.

Put all the sauce ingredients into a saucepan, season with salt and pepper and bring to the boil, stirring occasionally. Reduce the heat to a simmer. Put the meatballs into a steamer, cover with a tight-fitting lid and set the steamer over the pan. Steam for 10–15 minutes, until the meatballs are cooked through.

Transfer the meatballs to a serving dish and keep warm. Ladle the sauce into a blender or food processor and process until smooth. Pour the sauce over the meatballs and serve immediately with spaghetti, if using.

pork dim sum

SERVES 4

2 dried Chinese mushrooms
85 g/3 oz lean pork mince
2 tbsp drained canned chopped bamboo shoots
1 tsp light brown sugar
1 tsp sesame oil
½ tsp Chinese rice wine or dry sherry
1½ tsp soy sauce, plus extra to serve
1 tsp cornflour
chopped spring onion, to garnish

dumpling dough
150 g/5 oz self-raising flour, plus extra for dusting
50 ml/2 fl oz boiling water
1½ tsp groundnut oil

Put the dried mushrooms in a heatproof bowl, add hot water to cover and leave to soak for 20 minutes.

Meanwhile, make the dough. Sift the flour into a bowl and stir in the boiling water. Add the groundnut oil and 1–1½ tbsp cold water and mix to a dough. Turn out onto a lightly floured surface and knead until smooth. Divide the dough into 16 equal pieces and press out into rounds or squares.

Drain the mushrooms and finely chop. Mix together the mushrooms, pork, bamboo shoots, sugar, sesame oil, rice wine, soy sauce and cornflour in a bowl.

Divide the filling between the dough shapes, placing it in the centre of each. Pinch the edges of the dough together to make little pouches.

Bring a saucepan of water to the boil and line a steamer with damp greaseproof paper.

Put the pouches in a single layer in the steamer and cover with a tight-fitting lid. Set the steamer over the pan and steam for 10–15 minutes. Serve immediately, garnished with chopped spring onion and with a small dish of soy sauce for dipping.

lamb & bean stew

SERVES 4

225 g/8 oz black-eyed beans, soaked overnight in cold water and drained
3 tbsp sunflower oil
1 kg/2 lb 4 oz boneless leg of lamb, cut into cubes
4 leeks, sliced
1 parsnip, cut into cubes
3 carrots, thickly sliced
2 small turnips, cut into cubes
150 ml/5 fl oz beef stock
2 tbsp chopped fresh parsley
1 small fresh rosemary sprig
1 tbsp mint or redcurrant jelly
salt and pepper

Put the beans into a saucepan, add cold water to cover and bring to the boil. Boil vigorously for 15 minutes, then drain and set aside.

Heat the oil in a large frying pan. Add the meat and cook over a medium heat, stirring frequently, for about 8 minutes, until browned. Remove with a slotted spoon and set aside.

Add the leeks, parsnip, carrots and turnips to the pan and cook, stirring frequently, for about 8 minutes, until beginning to colour. Remove with a slotted spoon and set aside.

Pour the stock into the pan, add the herbs and mint jelly and bring to the boil, scraping up the sediment from the base. Remove from the heat.

Bring a saucepan of water to the boil. Mix together the lamb, vegetables and beans, season with salt and pepper and spoon into a 1.2-litre/2-pint pudding basin. Pour in the stock mixture. Cut a circle of foil 5 cm/2 inches larger than the circumference of the top of the basin, make a pleat in the centre and put it over the basin. Tie in place with string.

Put the basin into a steamer, cover with a tight-fitting lid and set it over the pan. Steam for 1¾ hours.

Transfer the lamb, vegetables and beans to a warmed serving dish with a slotted spoon. Remove and discard the rosemary sprig. Pour the liquid into a saucepan and boil until reduced. Pour over the stew and serve immediately.

herbed leg of lamb with vegetables

SERVES 6

1 tbsp sunflower oil
1 onion, thinly sliced
2 leeks, thinly sliced
2 carrots, thinly sliced
2 celery sticks, thinly sliced
1.5-kg/3 lb 5-oz leg of lamb, boned
4 garlic cloves, thinly sliced
2 fresh rosemary sprigs, plus extra to garnish
150 ml/5 fl oz beef stock
50 ml/2 fl oz rosé wine
2 tbsp mint or redcurrant jelly
salt and pepper

Cut a sheet of foil large enough to enclose the lamb completely. Heat the oil in a frying pan. Add the onion, leeks, carrots and celery and cook over a low heat, stirring occasionally, for 5 minutes. Using a slotted spoon, transfer the vegetables to the foil to make an even bed.

Meanwhile, make small slits all over the lamb with a small sharp knife. Push a slice of garlic and a few rosemary leaves into each slit.

Add the lamb to the pan, increase the heat to medium and cook, turning occasionally, for about 8 minutes, until lightly browned. Put the lamb on top of the vegetables. Fold up the sides of the foil but do not seal the parcel.

Pour the stock into the pan and bring to the boil, scraping up the sediment from the base. Add the wine and mint jelly and season with salt and pepper. Spoon the stock mixture over the lamb and seal the edges of the foil. Place the parcel in a steamer and cover with a tight-fitting lid.

Bring a saucepan of water to the boil. Set the steamer over the pan and steam for 1½ hours.

Remove the parcel from the steamer and unwrap. Put the lamb on a plate and leave to rest for 10–15 minutes. Meanwhile, tip the stock and vegetables into a saucepan and bring to a boil, then boil until reduced and thickened. Remove the pan from the heat.

Carve the lamb into medium-thick slices and place on a warmed serving dish. Spoon over the vegetables and sauce, garnish with rosemary and serve immediately.

spare ribs with black beans

SERVES 4

2 tbsp salted black beans
1 tbsp groundnut oil, plus extra for oiling
1 tbsp soy sauce
1 tbsp Chinese rice wine or dry sherry
1 tsp light brown sugar
1 tbsp cornflour
500 g/1 lb 2 oz pork spare ribs, chopped into short lengths
2 fresh red chillies, deseeded and sliced
1–2 garlic cloves, finely chopped

Put the beans into a bowl, add cold water to cover and leave to soak for 10 minutes, then drain well and mash with a fork.

Meanwhile, bring a saucepan of water to the boil and oil a heatproof dish that will fit inside the steamer.

Heat the oil in a frying pan or wok, add the beans and stir-fry for 1 minute. Add the soy sauce, rice wine and sugar and stir-fry for 30 seconds. Remove the pan from the heat and leave to cool.

Mix the cornflour to a paste with 2 tablespoons of cold water in a bowl. When the beans are cold, add the pieces of spare rib, cornflour paste, chillies and garlic and mix well.

Put the mixture into the prepared dish and place in a steamer. Cover with a tight-fitting lid, set the steamer over the pan of boiling water and steam for 30 minutes, until tender. Serve immediately.

chicken & leek parcels

SERVES 4

4 skinless, boneless chicken breast portions
1 fresh sage sprig
2 tbsp olive oil
2 tbsp walnut oil
4 tbsp lime juice
2 leeks, thinly sliced
4 tbsp chopped mixed fresh herbs, such as sage, flat-leaf parsley and thyme
2 garlic cloves, finely chopped
8 black olives, stoned and chopped
8 capers, chopped
salt and pepper

Put the chicken in a shallow non-metallic dish and add the sage sprig. Mix together the olive oil, walnut oil and lime juice in a bowl and pour the mixture over the chicken. Turn to coat, then cover with clingfilm and leave to marinate in the refrigerator for 2–4 hours. Meanwhile, cut out 4 sheets of foil, each large enough to enclose a chicken portion completely.

Bring a saucepan of water to the boil. Meanwhile, divide the leeks equally between the sheets of foil. Drain the chicken portions, reserving the marinade but discarding the sage sprig, and season them with salt and pepper. Place one on each pile of leeks.

Mix together the chopped herbs, garlic, olives and capers in a small bowl and divide the mixture between the parcels, spooning it on top of the chicken portions. Fold up the sides of the foil without sealing the edges and spoon in the reserved marinade.

Seal the edges of the parcels and place in a steamer. Cover with a tight-fitting lid and steam over the pan of boiling water for 15–20 minutes, until the chicken is cooked through and tender. Transfer the parcels to warmed individual serving plates, open the tops slightly and serve immediately.

chicken spirals with blue cheese sauce

SERVES 4

4 chicken breast portions
4 tsp sun-dried tomato purée
12 fresh basil leaves, plus extra to garnish
2 garlic cloves, finely chopped
2 tbsp snipped fresh chives
25 g/1 oz butter
salt and pepper

blue cheese sauce

175 g/6 oz dolcelatte cheese, crumbled
600 ml/1 pint crème fraîche
1 tbsp balsamic vinegar
1 tomato, peeled, deseeded and finely chopped
½ red pepper, deseeded and finely chopped

One at a time, put the chicken breasts between 2 sheets of clingfilm or greaseproof paper and beat gently with the side of a rolling pin to flatten. Season each with salt and pepper, then spread them evenly with the sun-dried tomato purée. Divide the basil leaves between them, then sprinkle with garlic and chives.

Bring a saucepan of water to the boil. Meanwhile, roll up each chicken breast, spread with butter and wrap in foil to hold securely. Put all the parcels into a steamer and cover with a tight-fitting lid. Set the steamer over the pan of boiling water and steam for 30–40 minutes, until cooked through and tender.

Remove the rolls from the steamer and set aside to cool completely, still wrapped in the foil.

To make the sauce, put the cheese, crème fraîche and balsamic vinegar into a blender and process until smooth. Alternatively, beat well in a bowl. Stir in the tomato and red pepper and season to taste with salt and pepper. Cover and chill until required.

When the chicken rolls are completely cold, unwrap and cut into slices. Spoon the sauce onto individual plates and top with the chicken spirals. Garnish with basil leaves and serve immediately.

duck breasts with apple & plum sauce

SERVES 4

2 crisp eating apples
lemon juice, for brushing
250 g/9 oz plums, stoned and halved
1 red onion, finely chopped
6 back peppercorns, lightly crushed
6 juniper berries, lightly crushed
600 ml/1 pint red wine
1 tbsp slivovitz, Calvados or brandy
4 duck breasts
1 tbsp sunflower oil
4 tbsp double cream
150 ml/5 fl oz chicken stock
salt

Peel and core the apples, then brush with lemon juice to prevent discoloration. Put them into a shallow dish with the plums, onion, peppercorns, juniper berries, red wine and slivovitz and mix well. Add the duck breasts and turn to coat. Leave to marinate in the refrigerator, turning the duck breasts occasionally, for 3 hours.

Drain the duck, reserving the marinade, and pat dry with kitchen paper. Heat the oil in a heavy-based frying pan, add the duck and cook over a medium heat for about 3 minutes on each side, until golden brown. Remove from the pan.

Put the duck breasts, apples and plums in a steamer and cover with a tight-fitting lid. Pour the remaining marinade into a saucepan, stir in the cream and chicken stock, bring to the boil and boil until thickened and reduced. Meanwhile, set the steamer over the pan and steam for 12–15 minutes.

Transfer the duck breasts to warmed serving plates. Slice the apples and add them to the plates with the plums. Keep warm. Bring the wine mixture back to the boil, season to taste with salt and strain. Spoon the sauce over the duck and serve immediately.

vegetables

creamy mushrooms with shallot sauce

SERVES 4

- 2 tbsp sunflower oil, plus extra for brushing
- 1 small onion, finely chopped
- 500 g/1 lb 2 oz chestnut mushrooms, chopped
- 55 g/2 oz fresh white breadcrumbs
- 2 eggs, lightly beaten
- 150 ml/5 fl oz soured cream
- salt and pepper
- fresh parsley sprigs, to garnish

shallot sauce

- 4 shallots, finely chopped
- 4 tbsp red wine vinegar
- 55 g/2 oz butter
- 25 g/1 oz plain flour
- 300 ml/10 fl oz vegetable stock
- 1 tsp lemon juice
- 2 tsp chopped fresh parsley
- salt and pepper

Heat the oil in a frying pan. Add the onion and cook over a low heat, stirring occasionally, for 10 minutes. Add the mushrooms and cook, stirring occasionally, for 5 minutes, until the juices have evaporated. Remove the pan from the heat and leave to cool slightly.

Meanwhile, bring a saucepan of water to the boil and brush a 600 ml/1 pint pudding basin with oil. Cut out a large round of greaseproof paper.

Stir the breadcrumbs, egg and cream into the mushroom mixture and season. Spoon the mixture into the basin, cover with the paper and tie in place.

Place the basin in a steamer and cover with a tight-fitting lid. Set the steamer over the pan of boiling water and steam for 1 hour.

Begin making the sauce about halfway through the cooking time. Put the shallots and vinegar into a saucepan and bring to the boil. Boil until the vinegar has almost evaporated. Add half the butter and, when it has melted, stir in the flour. Cook, stirring constantly, for 1 minute, then gradually stir in the stock. Bring to the boil, whisking constantly, then reduce the heat and simmer for 15 minutes.

Remove the sauce from the heat and season with salt and pepper. Whisk in the remaining butter and the lemon juice. Stir in the parsley.

Remove the mushroom mould from the steamer and discard the paper. Turn out the mould, garnish with parsley and serve immediately with the sauce.

summer vegetable parcels

SERVES 4

12 baby onions
12 baby carrots
12 radishes
115 g/4 oz mangetout
115 g/4 oz shelled baby broad beans
2 tsp chopped fresh mint
2 tsp chopped fresh parsley
2 tsp finely grated orange rind
4 tbsp dry white wine
55 g/2 oz butter
salt and pepper
crusty bread, to serve

Peel and trim the vegetables, as necessary. Bring a saucepan of water to the boil.

Meanwhile, cut out 4 double thickness rounds of greaseproof paper about 30 cm/12 inches in diameter. Divide the vegetables equally between them, placing them on one half of each round. Season with salt and pepper.

Sprinkle with the mint, parsley, orange rind and wine and dot with the butter. Fold the paper over and twist the edges to seal. Place the parcels in a steamer and cover with a tight-fitting lid.

Set the steamer over the pan of boiling water and steam for 10 minutes. Transfer the parcels to individual serving plates and serve immediately with crusty bread.

marinated vegetable medley

SERVES 4

1 Spanish onion, cut into wedges
1 aubergine, cut into chunks
1 orange pepper, deseeded and cut into chunks
2 courgettes, thickly sliced
1 butternut squash, peeled and cut into cubes
16 small mushrooms
150 ml/5 fl oz tomato juice
juice of 1 lemon
4 tbsp sunflower oil
1 tbsp Worcestershire sauce
1 fresh red chilli, deseeded and finely chopped
2 garlic cloves, finely chopped
1 tsp grated horseradish
½ tsp celery seeds
2 tsp chopped fresh thyme
1 tbsp chopped fresh parsley
300 ml/10 fl oz vegetable stock
salt and pepper

Put the onion, aubergine, orange pepper, courgettes, squash and mushrooms into a large dish. Mix the tomato juice, lemon juice, sunflower oil, Worcestershire sauce, chilli, garlic, horseradish, celery seeds, thyme and parsley together in a bowl and season with salt and pepper. Pour the mixture over the vegetables and toss to coat. Cover the dish with clingfilm and leave to marinate in the refrigerator for 4 hours.

Drain the vegetables, reserving the marinade. Pour the marinade into a saucepan, add the stock and bring to the boil.

Meanwhile, thread the vegetables on to 8 skewers and put them into a steamer. Cover with a tight-fitting lid, set the steamer over the pan of boiling water and steam for 8–10 minutes, until the vegetables are tender.

Transfer the skewers to a warmed serving dish. Check the consistency of the marinade and, if it is too thin, boil for a few minutes longer to reduce. Pour the marinade into a sauceboat and serve immediately with the kebabs.

harvesters' pie

SERVES 4

- 1 small onion, finely chopped
- 1 parsnip, finely chopped
- 1 small turnip, finely chopped
- 115 g/4 oz mushrooms, chopped
- 115 g/4 oz drained canned haricot beans
- 175 g/6 oz Cheddar or Gruyère cheese, grated
- 1 tsp chopped fresh thyme
- 2 tbsp plain flour
- 4 tbsp vegetable stock
- salt and pepper

pastry

- 175 g/6 oz plain flour, plus extra for dusting
- 1 tsp baking powder
- pinch of salt
- 85 g/3 oz butter, diced
- 1 egg, lightly beaten

First make the pastry. Sift together the flour, baking powder and salt into a bowl. Add the butter and rub in with your fingertips until the mixture resembles fine breadcrumbs. Stir in the egg and just enough water to mix to a firm dough.

Turn out onto a lightly floured surface and knead briefly. Cut off and reserve a quarter of the pastry and roll out the remainder. Use the larger piece of pastry to line an 850-ml/1½-pint pudding basin, easing it gently into place. Roll out the smaller piece of pastry to make a lid.

Half fill a saucepan with water and bring to the boil. Cut out a round of greaseproof paper and a round of foil 5 cm/2 inches larger than the top of the basin. Place them together and make a pleat in the centre.

Mix together the onion, parsnip, turnip, mushrooms, beans and cheese in a bowl. Sprinkle with the thyme and flour, season with salt and pepper and mix well. Spoon the mixture into the lined basin, pressing it down gently. Add the vegetable stock and cover with the pastry lid. Put the greaseproof paper and foil rounds over the basin and tie securely with kitchen string.

Carefully put the basin into the boiling water, which should come about halfway up the side. Cover the pan with a tight-fitting lid and steam for 3 hours.

Lift the basin out of the pan. Discard the cover and turn out the pie. Serve immediately.

focaccia with tomatoes & taleggio

SERVES 4

- 1 onion, cheese or herb focaccia
- 1 tbsp pesto
- 55 g/2 oz unsalted butter, at room temperature
- 2 large ripe plum tomatoes, peeled and thinly sliced
- 140 g/5 oz Taleggio cheese, thinly sliced
- 3 eggs
- 300 ml/10 fl oz single cream
- 1 tbsp chopped fresh flat-leaf parsley
- 55 g/2 oz Parmesan cheese, grated
- salt and pepper

Slice the focaccia. Beat the pesto and butter together in a small bowl, then spread the mixture over one side of each slice of bread.

Make layers of focaccia, tomatoes and Taleggio cheese in a heatproof dish that will fit inside the steamer. Lightly beat the eggs in a bowl, then beat in the cream, add the parsley and season with salt and pepper. Pour the mixture evenly over the contents of the dish and leave to stand for 30 minutes.

Bring a saucepan of water to the boil. Cover the dish with foil and put it in the steamer. Cover with a tight-fitting lid and set over the pan. Steam for 40 minutes.

Towards the end of the cooking time, preheat the grill. Lift the dish out of the steamer and remove and discard the foil. Sprinkle the Parmesan cheese over the surface, place under the grill and cook for a few minutes, until golden brown and bubbling.

courgette & carrot terrine

SERVES 6

- 2 tbsp groundnut oil, plus extra for brushing
- 225 g/8 oz onions, chopped
- 2 garlic cloves, finely chopped
- 1 kg/2 lb 4 oz courgettes, grated
- 175 g/6 oz carrots, diced
- 750 g/1 lb 10 oz pak choi
- 1 tbsp soy sauce
- pinch of dried chillies
- 115 g/4 oz day-old breadcrumbs
- 4 egg whites, lightly beaten

Heat the oil in a frying pan. Add the onions, garlic and courgettes and cook over a low heat, stirring occasionally, for 12 minutes, until beginning to colour. Increase the heat and cook for a further 5 minutes. Remove from the heat and set aside to cool.

Put the carrots in a saucepan, add water to cover and bring to the boil. Reduce the heat and simmer for 7 minutes. Drain, refresh under cold water and pat dry with kitchen paper. Bring a saucepan of water to the boil, add the pak choi and blanch for 1 minute. Drain well and chop.

Put half the courgettes, the pak choi, soy sauce and chillies into a food processor and process to a purée. Add the breadcrumbs and process briefly. Transfer to a bowl and stir in the remaining courgettes and the egg whites.

Bring a saucepan of water to the boil. Line a terrine or loaf tin with greaseproof paper and brush lightly with oil. Spoon one third of the courgettes into the terrine and spread out. Add half the carrots, then half the remaining courgettes. Top with the remaining carrots and spread the remaining courgettes over them.

Brush a piece of greaseproof paper with oil and place it on top. Cover with foil, secured with kitchen string. Put the terrine into a steamer and cover with a tight-fitting lid. Set the steamer over the pan of boiling water and steam for 1½ hours.

Remove the terrine and leave to cool, then chill in the refrigerator for 8 hours or overnight. Discard the coverings, turn out onto a serving plate and discard the lining paper. Cut into slices to serve.

spinach & gorgonzola ravioli

SERVES 4

pasta dough
350 g/12 oz strong white bread flour, plus extra for dusting
½ tsp salt
2 eggs
1 tbsp olive oil

filling
225 g/8 oz spinach, trimmed
25 g/1 oz butter
2 shallots, finely chopped
55 g/2 oz Gorgonzola cheese, crumbled
40 g/1½ oz pecorino cheese, grated, plus extra to serve
pinch of grated nutmeg
salt and pepper

To make the pasta dough, sift the flour and salt into a bowl and make a well in the centre. Add the eggs, olive oil and 2 tablespoons of water to the well and, using your hands, gradually incorporate the dry ingredients to make an elastic dough, adding 1 tablespoon of water if necessary. Turn the dough out on to a lightly floured surface and knead well until smooth. Put into a plastic bag and leave to rest in the refrigerator for 15 minutes.

Cook the spinach in a little water for 4 minutes or until just wilted. Drain and chop. Melt the butter in a pan. Cook the shallots for 5 minutes, stirring frequently. Add the spinach, cheeses, parsley and nutmeg. Season and leave to cool.

Halve the pasta dough. Roll out one half on a lightly floured surface to about 3 mm/⅛ inch thick. Brush it lightly with water, then place heaped teaspoonfuls of the filling at regular intervals over it. Roll out the other piece of dough and put it on top. With floured fingers, gently press the top sheet down around the mounds of filling to seal. Cut out the ravioli with a fluted pasta cutter or a fluted biscuit cutter.

Bring a large saucepan of salted water to the boil. Add the ravioli, bring back to the boil and cook for 5 minutes. Drain well and refresh under cold water. Put into a heatproof dish or bowl that will fit inside the steamer.

Cover the steamer with a tight-fitting lid, set it over the pan of boiling water and steam for 15 minutes. Transfer the ravioli to a warmed serving plate, garnish with parsley sprigs and serve immediately.

chickpeas & vegetables

SERVES 4

- 225 g/8 oz dried chickpeas, soaked overnight in cold water to cover and drained
- 2 tbsp olive oil
- 1 onion, chopped
- 1 garlic clove, chopped
- 2 celery sticks, chopped
- 2 carrots, chopped
- 1 green pepper, deseeded and chopped
- 1 red pepper, deseeded and chopped
- 1 small celeriac, chopped
- 500 g/1 lb 2 oz tomatoes, peeled and chopped, or 400 g/14 oz canned chopped tomatoes
- 115 g/4 oz bulgar wheat
- pinch of grated nutmeg
- pinch of ground cloves
- ½ tsp ground ginger
- salt and pepper

Put the chickpeas in a large saucepan, add cold water to cover and bring to the boil, then reduce the heat and simmer for 1½ hours.

Meanwhile, heat the olive oil in a large frying pan. Add the onion and garlic and cook over a low heat, stirring occasionally, for 5 minutes, until soft. Add the celery, carrots, green and red peppers and celeriac and cook, stirring occasionally, for a further 5 minutes. Stir in the tomatoes, bulgar wheat, nutmeg, cloves and ginger and bring to the boil. Remove the pan from the heat.

Season the vegetables with salt and pepper and spoon them into a 1.2-litre/2-pint pudding basin. Put the basin into a steamer and cover with a tight-fitting lid. Set the steamer over the pan of chickpeas and steam for 45 minutes, adding more boiling water to the chickpeas, as necessary.

Remove the steamer and drain the chickpeas. Stir them into the vegetables and taste and adjust the seasoning. Transfer to a warmed serving dish and serve immediately.

side dishes

chilli potatoes

SERVES 4

500 g/1 lb 2 oz new potatoes
3 dried red chillies
1 tbsp hot paprika
1 tsp ground cumin
2 garlic cloves, chopped
½ tsp salt
2 tbsp sherry vinegar
150 ml/5 fl oz olive oil

Bring a saucepan of water to the boil. Put the unpeeled potatoes into a steamer, cover with a tight-fitting lid and set the steamer over the pan. Steam for about 20 minutes, until tender.

Pound the chillies, paprika and cumin to a paste in a mortar with a pestle. Add the garlic and salt and continue to pound until fully incorporated. Gradually stir in the vinegar, then whisk in the oil, a little at a time.

When the potatoes are tender, remove them from the steamer and peel if you like. Put them into a warmed serving dish, pour the sauce over them and serve immediately.

pilau rice

SERVES 4

- 225 g/8 oz basmati rice, rinsed and soaked
- 2 tbsp sunflower oil
- 2 garlic cloves, finely chopped
- 1 onion, finely chopped
- 1 fresh red chilli, deseeded and finely chopped
- 1 red pepper, deseeded and finely chopped
- 1 tsp ground cumin
- ½ tsp ground turmeric
- 1 tsp fennel seeds
- ½ tsp ground coriander
- 2 green cardamom pods, lightly crushed
- 2 cloves
- about 450 ml/15 fl oz vegetable or chicken stock or water
- salt and pepper
- fresh coriander sprigs, to garnish

Drain the rice well and set aside. Heat the oil in a saucepan. Add the garlic, onion, chilli and red pepper and cook over a low heat, stirring occasionally, for 5 minutes, until soft. Stir in the cumin, turmeric, fennel seeds, coriander, cardamom and cloves and cook, stirring constantly, for 1 minute, until the spices give off their aroma.

Add the rice and cook, stirring constantly, for 2–3 minutes, until opaque. Pour in the stock and season with salt and pepper. Bring to the boil, then reduce the heat to very low, cover with a tight-fitting lid and steam for 20 minutes, until all the liquid has been absorbed. Do not remove the lid during cooking.

Remove the saucepan from the heat and leave to stand, without removing the lid, for 2 minutes. Uncover and fluff up the grains with a fork. Transfer to a warmed serving dish and remove and discard the cloves and cardamom pods. Garnish with coriander sprigs and serve immediately.

spiced saffron rice

SERVES 6

about 450 ml/15 fl oz vegetable stock or water
½ tsp saffron threads, lightly crushed
rice
1 tbsp sunflower oil
225 g/8 oz basmati rice, rinsed and soaked
½ tsp salt
4 green cardamom pods

Put 3 tablespoons of the stock into a small saucepan, add the saffron and heat gently to simmering point. Remove the pan from the heat and set aside.

Drain the rice. Heat the oil in a large saucepan. Add the rice and cook, stirring constantly, for 2–3 minutes, until opaque. Pour in the stock and season with salt and pepper, add the salt and cardamom pods. Bring to the boil, then reduce the heat to very low, cover with a tight-fitting lid and steam for 15 minutes. Do not remove the lid during steaming.

Add the saffron and its soaking liquid to the pan, re-cover and steam for a further 5–7 minutes, until all the liquid has been absorbed.

Remove the pan from the heat and leave to stand, without removing the lid, for 2 minutes. Uncover the rice and fluff up the grains with a fork. Remove and discard the cardamom pods and serve immediately.

bulgar wheat with herbs

SERVES 4

25 g/1 oz butter
½ red onion, finely chopped
1 garlic clove, finely chopped
175 g/6 oz bulgar wheat
1 bay leaf
475 ml/16 fl oz vegetable stock or chicken stock
4 tbsp chopped fresh parsley
4 tbsp chopped fresh mint
3 spring onions, finely chopped
55 g/2 oz black olives
175 g/6 oz cherry tomatoes, halved
125 ml/4 fl oz extra virgin olive oil
4 tbsp lemon juice
salt and pepper
fresh mint sprigs, to garnish

Melt the butter in a saucepan. Add the onion and garlic and cook over a low heat, stirring occasionally, for 5 minutes, until soft. Add the bulgar wheat and bay leaf, pour in the stock and bring to the boil. Reduce the heat to very low, cover with a tight-fitting lid and steam for 15 minutes, until all the liquid has been absorbed.

Remove the pan from the heat and spoon the bulgar wheat mixture into a bowl. Remove and discard the bay leaf. Leave to cool slightly, then add the parsley, mint, spring onions, black olives and tomatoes. Mix well.

Whisk together the olive oil and lemon juice in a jug and season with salt and pepper. Pour the dressing into the bowl and toss to mix. Serve at room temperature, garnished with mint sprigs.

couscous with nuts & dried fruit

SERVES 6

250 g/9 oz couscous
600 ml/1 pint water
70 g/2½ oz ready-to-eat dried apricots
40 g/1½ oz blanched almonds
600 ml/1 pint vegetable stock, chicken stock or water
1 tsp extra virgin olive oil
2 tbsp chopped fresh coriander
salt and pepper

Put the couscous into a bowl and pour in the water. Leave to soak, stirring frequently with a fork to separate the grains, for 30 minutes, until almost all the liquid has been absorbed.

Meanwhile, using a sharp knife, cut the apricots into thin strips and set aside. Heat a heavy-based frying pan, add the almonds and cook over a low heat, shaking the pan frequently, for 1–2 minutes, until lightly toasted. Remove the pan from the heat.

Pour the stock into a saucepan and bring to the boil. Line a steamer with muslin. Stir the apricots into the soaked couscous, season with salt and pepper and spoon into the steamer. Cover with a tight-fitting lid, set the steamer over the pan and steam for 20 minutes.

Transfer the couscous mixture to a warmed serving dish and stir in the olive oil, coriander and almonds. Serve immediately.

peas with lettuce, shallots & mint

SERVES 6

500 g/1 lb 2 oz shelled fresh peas
2 shallots, thinly sliced
1 garlic clove, finely chopped
8 cos lettuce leaves, shredded
3 fresh mint sprigs
1 tsp caster sugar
25 g/1 oz butter or
2 tbsp sunflower oil
salt and pepper

Bring a saucepan of water to the boil. Line a steamer with dampened greaseproof paper.

Put the peas into the steamer and add the shallots, garlic, lettuce and mint sprigs. Sprinkle with the sugar and dot with the butter. Season with salt and pepper.

Cover the steamer with a tight-fitting lid and set the steamer over the pan of boiling water. Steam for about 4–5 minutes, until the peas are tender.

Remove and discard the mint sprigs. Transfer the vegetables to a warmed serving dish and serve immediately.

glazed carrots & parsnips

SERVES 6

600 ml/1 pint vegetable stock or water
3 tbsp clear honey
4 tbsp toasted sesame seeds
16 baby carrots, topped and tailed
8 baby parsnips, topped and tailed
salt and pepper

Pour the stock into a large saucepan and bring to the boil. Meanwhile, pour the honey into a small saucepan and heat gently until just warm. Alternatively, heat briefly in a bowl in the microwave. Remove from the heat.

Spread out the sesame seeds on a shallow plate. Brush the carrots and parsnips all over with the honey, then roll them in the sesame seeds.

Put the vegetables in a steamer in a single layer and cover with a tight-fitting lid. Set the steamer over the pan of boiling water and steam for 20–25 minutes, until the vegetables are tender. Serve immediately.

desserts

rich crème brûlée with exotic fruit

SERVES 6

450 ml/16 fl oz double cream
4 egg yolks
2 tbsp caster sugar
½ tsp vanilla extract
1 banana
lemon juice, for brushing
1 small mango, peeled, stoned and chopped
2 kiwi fruit, peeled and chopped
2 tbsp chopped stem ginger
55 g/2 oz demerara sugar

Pour the cream into a small saucepan and bring to just below boiling point. Meanwhile, beat together the egg yolks and caster sugar until pale and creamy. Gradually stir in the cream until thoroughly combined, then stir in the vanilla extract.

Bring a saucepan of water to the boil. Meanwhile, peel the banana, brush with lemon juice and slice into a bowl. Add the mango, kiwi fruit and ginger and mix well.

Divide the fruit equally between 6 ramekins, then pour over the egg custard. Cover the ramekins with clingfilm, put in a steamer and cover with a tight-fitting lid. Set the steamer over the pan of boiling water and steam for 15–20 minutes, until set.

Remove the ramekins from the steamer and remove and discard the clingfilm, then leave to cool. Cover with fresh clingfilm and chill in the refrigerator for at least 4 hours.

Preheat the grill. Remove and discard the clingfilm and sprinkle the sugar over the top of the desserts. Place the ramekins under the grill for 2–3 minutes, until the tops are caramelized and golden, turning occasionally so that they brown evenly. Chill in the refrigerator for at least 2 hours, until the caramel is crisp.

light-as-air fresh fruit sponge with hot fruit coulis

SERVES 4

5 mandarin oranges
sunflower oil, for brushing
2 tsp golden syrup
1 banana
1 tsp lemon juice
150 g/5½ oz self-raising flour
25 g/1 oz finely ground Brazil nuts
85 g/3 oz fresh white breadcrumbs
85 g/3 oz caster sugar
7 tbsp milk

hot fruit coulis
2 passion fruit
1 mango, peeled, stoned and chopped
6 tbsp mandarin juice

Finely grate the rind of 2 mandarins and squeeze out the juice. Peel the remaining mandarins, removing all traces of pith. Cut them into thin slices with a sharp knife.

Brush a 1-litre/1¾-pint pudding basin with oil and spoon in the golden syrup. Arrange the mandarin slices in the basin and set aside. Bring a saucepan of water to the boil.

Peel the banana and mash with the lemon juice. Sift the flour into a bowl and stir in the nuts, breadcrumbs, sugar and grated rind. Stir in the milk and enough juice to make a firm mixture. Spoon into the basin and level the top.

Cut out circles of greaseproof paper and foil, 5 cm/2 inches larger than the top of the basin, put them together and make a pleat in the centre. Cover the basin, foil side uppermost, and tie in place. Put the basin in a steamer and cover with a tight-fitting lid. Set over the pan of boiling water and steam for 1¾ hours.

Meanwhile, make the coulis. Halve the passion fruit and scoop out the pulp and seeds into a blender or food processor. Add the mango, mandarin juice and 3 tablespoons of water. Process until smooth. Pass the coulis through a nylon sieve into a bowl and set aside.

Just before serving, gently heat the coulis in a small saucepan. Remove the sponge from the steamer, discard the covering and turn out. Serve, handing around the hot coulis separately.

hazelnut cloud

SERVES 4

unsalted butter, for greasing
4 eggs, separated
125 g/4½ oz caster sugar
300 ml/10 fl oz double cream
115 g/4 oz ground hazelnuts
finely grated rind of 1 lemon
pinch of ground allspice

Generously grease a 15-cm/6-inch soufflé dish with butter. Cut a double strip of greaseproof paper long enough to go around the circumference of the dish with a 5-cm/2-inch overlap and deep enough to stand 5 cm/2 inches above the rim. Tie the strip around the outside of the dish with kitchen string.

Using an electric mixer, beat together the egg yolks and caster sugar until pale and creamy and the whisk leaves a ribbon trail when it is lifted. Pour in the cream and whisk until thickened. Fold in the hazelnuts, lemon rind and allspice.

Stiffly whisk the egg whites in a grease-free bowl, then gently fold into the egg yolk mixture with a flexible spatula. Gently scrape the mixture into the prepared soufflé dish.

Put the dish into a large saucepan and pour in enough boiling water to come about halfway up the side. Cover with a tight-fitting lid and steam very gently for 45 minutes.

Lift the basin out of the pan. Remove and discard the paper collar and serve immediately.

pears in red wine sauce

SERVES 4

grated rind and juice of 1 orange
300 ml/10 fl oz red wine
3 tbsp clear honey
1 cinnamon stick
1 vanilla pod
½ tsp mixed spice
1 clove
4 firm, ripe pears
½ tsp arrowroot or potato flour
whipped cream, to serve (optional)

Bring a saucepan of water to the boil. Meanwhile, put the orange rind and juice, wine, honey, cinnamon stick, vanilla pod, spice and clove in a saucepan and bring to the boil, stirring frequently, then remove the pan from the heat.

Peel the pears, leaving the stem intact, and cut off a small slice from the base so that they will stand upright. Put them into a heatproof bowl and pour the wine mixture over them. Cover the bowl with a sheet of foil and tie in place with kitchen string.

Put the bowl into the steamer and cover with a tight-fitting lid. Set the steamer over the pan and steam for 35–40 minutes, until the pears are tender.

Remove the bowl from the steamer and leave to cool completely. Transfer the pears to a serving dish, standing them upright. Remove and discard the cinnamon stick, vanilla pod and clove from the wine mixture and pour it into a small saucepan. Bring to the boil and cook until reduced to about 150 ml/5 fl oz. Reduce the heat to a simmer.

Put the arrowroot into a small bowl and stir in 2 tablespoons of the wine sauce to make a paste. Stir the paste into the pan and simmer gently, stirring constantly, for 2 minutes, until the sauce has thickened. Remove the pan from the heat and leave to cool.

Pour the wine sauce over the pears and chill in the refrigerator for at least 3 hours before serving with whipped cream, if using.

traditional toffee pudding

SERVES 4–6

115 g/4 oz walnut halves
sunflower oil, for brushing
175 g/6 oz dark brown sugar
175 g/6 oz unsalted butter
4 tbsp double cream , plus extra for serving
2 tbsp lemon juice
2 eggs, lightly beaten
115 g/4 oz self-raising flour

Heat a heavy-based frying pan, add the walnuts and cook, shaking the pan frequently, for a few minutes, until lightly toasted. Remove the pan from the heat and leave to cool, then chop the nuts.

Brush an 850-ml/1½-pint pudding basin with oil. Sprinkle half the chopped walnuts over the base.

Put 55 g/2 oz of the sugar, 55 g/2 oz of the butter, the cream and half the lemon juice into a small saucepan and heat gently, stirring constantly, until the butter has melted, the sugar has dissolved and the mixture is smooth. Remove the pan from the heat and pour half the sauce into the basin, then swirl gently to coat the side. Reserve the remaining sauce in the pan.

Put the remaining sugar and butter into a bowl and beat until pale and fluffy. Gradually beat in the eggs, a little at a time. Sift the flour over the mixture and fold in with a flexible spatula, then fold in the remaining walnuts and lemon juice.

Bring a saucepan of water to the boil. Meanwhile, spoon the mixture into the basin. Cut out a circle of greaseproof paper 5 cm/2 inches larger than the circumference of the top of the basin. Make a pleat in the middle, cover the basin and tie in place with kitchen string.

Put the basin into a steamer, cover with a tight-fitting lid, place over the pan of boiling water and steam for 1½ hours. Just before you are ready to serve, reheat the remaining sauce until warm.

Remove and discard the greaseproof paper. Run a round-bladed knife around the inside of the basin, place a warmed serving plate on top and, holding them together, invert. Pour the remaining sauce over the pudding and serve immediately with double cream to accompany.

gooey chocolate & almond dessert

SERVES 6

125 g/4½ oz unsalted butter, plus extra for greasing
125 g/4½ oz caster sugar
6 day-old sponge fingers
85 g/3 oz plain chocolate, broken into pieces
6 eggs, separated
115 g/4 oz ground almonds
cream, to serve (optional)

chocolate & brandy sauce
55 g/2 oz unsalted butter
115 g/4 oz caster sugar
115 g/4 oz plain chocolate, broken into pieces
50 ml/2 fl oz milk
2 tbsp brandy

Bring a saucepan of water to the boil. Grease a 1.2-litre/2-pint pudding basin with butter and sprinkle with 1 tablespoon of the sugar. Break up the sponge fingers and crush.

Melt the chocolate in a heatproof bowl set over a saucepan of barely simmering water, stirring occasionally. Set aside to cool slightly.

Beat the remaining butter and the remaining sugar in a bowl until light and fluffy. Gradually beat in the egg yolks, then the chocolate. Fold in the crumbs and almonds. Stiffly whisk the egg whites and fold them into the mixture. Spoon into the basin and smooth the surface.

Cut out circles of greaseproof paper and foil 5 cm/2 inches larger than the circumference of the top of the basin and put them together. Grease the paper and make a pleat in the centre of both circles. Cover the basin, foil side uppermost, and tie in place with kitchen string. Put it into a steamer, cover with a lid and set over the pan of boiling water. Steam for 1 hour.

To make the sauce, melt the butter and sugar in a small saucepan, stirring constantly. Remove from the heat. Melt the chocolate in a heatproof bowl set over a saucepan of simmering water. Stir in the butter mixture, then gradually stir in the milk, 50 ml/2 fl oz water and the brandy. Remove from the heat.

Lift the basin out of the steamer and discard the coverings. Turn out the dessert, pour over the sauce, and serve with cream, if using.

chocolate & cherry delights

SERVES 4

125 g/4½ oz unsalted butter, softened, plus extra for greasing
115 g/4 oz dark brown sugar
1 ripe pear
100 g/3½ oz black cherries, stoned and halved
85 g/3 oz plain flour
3 tbsp cocoa powder
½ tsp baking powder
2 eggs, lightly beaten
1 tsp kirsch
2 tbsp clear honey
115 g/4 oz plain chocolate

Bring a saucepan of water to the boil. Generously grease 4 individual pudding basins, about 250 ml/8 fl oz each, with butter. Sprinkle a little sugar in each to coat all over the insides and tip out any excess.

Peel, core and dice the pear and put it into a bowl. Add the cherries and mix well. Divide the fruit equally between the prepared basins.

Sift together the flour, cocoa powder and baking powder into a large bowl and add the remaining sugar, 115 g/4 oz of the butter and the eggs. Beat well with an electric mixer until thoroughly combined and smooth.

Spoon the mixture into the basins, dividing it equally between them. Cut out 4 greaseproof paper and 4 foil circles 4 cm/1½ inches larger than the circumference of the tops of the basins. Hold the circles together, make a pleat in the middle and cover the basins, foil circle uppermost. Tie in place with kitchen string.

Put the basins in a steamer and cover with a tight-fitting lid. Set the steamer over the pan of boiling water and steam for 45 minutes.

Just before the end of the cooking time, put the remaining butter in a small saucepan with the kirsch and honey. Break the chocolate into pieces and add to the pan, then heat gently, stirring constantly, until melted and smooth.

Lift the basin out of the steamer and discard the covers. Run a knife around the basins to loosen, and then turn out. Pour the sauce over the desserts and serve immediately.